ADMISSIONS

donnarkevic

FUTURECYCLE PRESS

Mineral Bluff, Georgia

Published by FutureCycle Press
Mineral Bluff, Georgia, USA

ISBN 978-1-938853-03-6

To Emercine and Joe

∞

Thanks to Frank Montesonti and Diane Kistner

Some of them have left behind a name
that is remembered to their praise;
but of others there is no memory...
and they are as though they never lived.

Sirach 44:8-9

To be a child again is to go forward—
And that is much to know. Many grow old,
And fade, and go away, not knowing how much
That is to know. Mary, the night is coming,
And there will soon be darkness all around you.
Let us go down where Martha waits for us,
And let there be light shining in this house.

From "Lazarus," by Edwin Arlington Robinson

TABLE OF CONTENTS

West Virginia Hospital for the Insane, 1864..................................... 9

Medicine to Prevent Conception... 11

Grief.. 13

Sexual Abuse.. 15

Exposure..18

Staff Slaughterhouse Worker: Josiah Cain..23

Novel Reading..24

Severe Labor..26

Loss of Leg...28

Snuff Eating.. 30

Carbuncle.. 32

Staff Sawmill Worker: Arby Persinger...35

Hard Study...37

Women Trouble...42

Remorse..45

Hereditary Predisposition... 46

Religious Excitement... 50

Staff Cook: Rosa... 53

Opium Habit...61

Bad Company...64

Staff Superintendent: Dr. R.T. Ferguson.. 65

Confinement... 67

Smallpox...71

Marriage of Son.. 74

Fighting Fire... 76

Staff Icehouse Worker: Amos Tandy... 80

Desertion By Husband..82

Gunshot Wound.. 83

Female Disease..86

Religious Enthusiasm...89

Suppression of Menses..91

Staff Laundry Foreman: Olis Cremeans.. 92

Explosion of Shell Nearby.. 94

Time of Life.. 96

WEST VIRGINIA HOSPITAL FOR THE INSANE, 1864

Citizens of Weston welcomed me:
glad-handing politicians, a brass band,
a thousand school children, faces spruced,
fresh as whitewashed fences.

But I am a city unto myself:

Out of the depths, through fissured rock,
spring waters feed the reservoir.
Next to the waterkeeper's cottage, sheep
graze under pastoral observation.
Barns and silo store enough to sustain
the body: bread, butter, milk, meat,
enough to survive the bare cupboard,
the winter of a kraaled soul.
In the arboretum, perpetual Gethsemane,
supplications rise like canticles
and fall on the ears of inferior gods,
Miserere nobis.

Inside the sawmill, harvested timber
submits to the saw:
debarked, canted, edged, trimmed, dried, planed.
From the abattoir,
the death squeals of hogs, sheep, cattle echo,
and the bone mound, a feral Golgotha, rises
next to the hominal slaughterhouse of histories.
In the icehouse, time stops.
Solid blocks of the West Fork River,
frozen pantomime of movement, chill milk,
meat, and arrest the decay of bodies,
waiting for winter to give ground.
On the edge of unmerchantable wood,
I scratch out final refuge, evidenced by

crude stone markers, nuisance weeds,
anonymous and fixed as stars.

Prisoners quarried me in Mount Clare,
delivered me in ox-drawn wagons,
my body, blue sandstone slabs, thick as time,
my head, slate, another sedimentary stone.
I am a thicket of halls and locked doors,
each single cell, a pod of mock seed,
growing like bittersweet vines, strangling
walls into a doxology of silence.

My countenance, a three-faced clock,
the father, son, and ghost of those committed,
marks every moment, while my heart, an iron bell,
pulses with the resident echo of inborn fracture.
Outside the barred windows, vagrant clouds escape
the reach of sycamores. As a wrought iron fence reins
the horizon, limbs conspire to cradle sky,
to bear deliverance in blossoms.

MEDICINE TO PREVENT CONCEPTION

```
            W. Va. Hospital for the Insane
            Name:    Danny Moser
            Admitted: 14 February, 1880
```

Like poison ivy it grows, a contagion
in the belly of my sweetheart,
Polly, too young for motherhood,
her Paw, too itchy on the trigger,
too good a shot.

For deliverance we pray
to a God who prefers creation.
We watch for a sign.
Polly starts to show.

To weed our Garden of Eden
I beg a one-eyed peddler,
the self-proclaimed savior of Shiloh.
He offers the cure for a double eagle.
I offer half and Daddy's war revolver.
Sucking on a peppermint stick,
he slides a bottle in my hand
cold as a creek trout, his smile,
like a cur's, one whiskered lip raised,
revealing the glint of a silver tooth.
He whispers, *Cures all. Tells none.*

Lonely as stars we lie awake.
At sunrise, in an abandoned barn,
the blue bottle swaddles in Polly's hands,
the liquid, thick as whitewash.
Like a baby rattle, her hands shake.
We kiss. She drinks.
On straw, foul with ancient afterbirth

we wait. Through weathered barn boards
sunrays dribble like a leaky churn.
A cock crows.
Polly grabs her stomach,
aching like a thousand catfights.
She throws up, her eyes roll back,
and she screams like her time come.

Like a bride over the threshold,
I carry Polly's body
to her Paw's parlor, her face
white as mother's milk,
his tears, unanswered prayers,
my mind broken, beyond repair,
like a horse with a fractured leg.

————

To prevent me from committing
the Judas-sin in this asylum,
they hog-tie me in a straightjacket.
For hours I rock like a baby.
But I am a patient spider.
From this web I have woven,
I am determined to hang.

GRIEF

```
W. Va. Hospital for the Insane
Name:     Jack Holt
Admitted: 7 May, 1881
```

In a coal town, death is expected.

From mother to mother,
like a swaddled infant,
news of a drowning passes.
The women take charge.
They linger over details,
the crafted patchwork
of a community quilt,
each attempting to identify
which of Jack's three boys...
Yes, a cousin confirms,
the youngest.

Women prepare too much food
delivered by their men,
posing on the front porch rail
like crows; Jack broods.
What more could a man do?
So much rain,
the river current stronger,
others assure, than any
father's arms.

At the viewing, women mourn
in groups, their children herded
'round them, stepping on the hems
of their mothers' black dresses
without being scolded.

In front of the coffin, Jack paces,
begging all comers to touch
the red furrows on his arms and hands,
the clawing of his son's frantic fingernails
fresh as stigmata.

At the cemetery, muddy runoff
from the night's rain
fills the grave knee-deep.
Jack jumps in.
With cupped hands, he bails,
refusing to get out
until five men yank him from the pit.
Thrashing as though caught in a deluge,
he bloodies a few noses until clubbed
unconscious with a pickaxe handle.

———

Every time the sound of rain
echoes on the slate roof of the asylum,
like the futile voice of a boy submerged,
the orderlies strap Jack down to the bed,
like mooring a boat
to weather an unforgiving storm.

SEXUAL ABUSE

W. Va. Hospital for the Insane
Name: Aaron Scott
Admitted: 3 June, 1887

8

Grandpa dips nickels in honey,
tells me I can earn them
by licking them off his palm
like sugar lumps he feeds horses.
Grandma, mending socks,
laughs, says, *Go ahead*
His hands are clean.
Your cousins done it for less.

9

In the barn. The smell
of silage, fodder, and manure.
Grandpa does it to me
the first time. His *horse,* he calls it.
My cob, he says, grinning,
his teeth rotted tree stumps,
his hands coarse as corn husks
I feed the hogs.

Grandma says, *You don't eat much*
more than a sparrow.
Even my favorite, biscuits and gravy,
makes me sick to my stomach,
like too much molasses at a candy pull.
Grandpa grins, says, *Why,*
once I seen him eat a horse.

10

Afterwards, afraid to touch
the gob, it scabs on my belly,

fractures light, glints
like a spider's web,
bits of me imprisoned
like ants in tree sap.

11

I don't know why, but one summer
I slingshot every sparrow
nesting in the barn eaves,
their worm-fat bodies
kerplump on the ground.
Jesus, I don't know why.

12

Wednesday night church-going.
Grandma gone. The fear of God
rises in my bedroom, sticking in my throat,
supplications failing, falling on heretic ears,
his silhouette in the door frame,
unholy picture.
Grandpa preys.

13

Like birds conspiring before sunrise
or assassins scheming,
I hear whisperings. I don't understand
why I hid one of Grandpa's
shotguns under my mattress,
its steel spine, a thin hump,
like the fresh grave of a child.

14

Just once I tell him, *No!*
He backhands me,
not too old for him yet,
his eyes like the hoot owl's

when I slap him back
and aim that stagecoach 10-gauge
at him. But that grin returns.
He thinks I don't have it in me.

———

In letters to me at the asylum,
Grandma says she prays
for both our souls and quotes scripture:
You are worth more than many sparrows.

Me, I don't believe.

EXPOSURE

```
        W. Va. Hospital for the Insane
        Name:    D. T. Ross
        Admitted: 24 February, 1884
```

An artist, I photograph Southern gentry.
To avoid conscription into the Confed Army,
I reproduce military maps, artless as a scrivener.
On orders, I travel sixty train-miles south
of Macon to Fort Sumter, a POW prison,
a forgettable pismire of a berg named
Andersonville.

Reveille

On horseback, Captain Wirz trots
a line of Yanks who have passed muster
for the last time. The rat-tat-tat
of a red-capped drummer, eager
but not old enough to man a sentry box,
summons the dead-wagon
while fights break out over dead men's rags.
After tying toes together, pariah dogs,
working for double rations, toss
naked bodies into the wain like cholera hogs.
Some men retain dead messmates,
for the roll count equals rations delivered.
As the vehicle jogs to the cemetery,
heads, arms, and legs bob.

0 a.m.

Officers pose: scabbards and sabers,
ostrich-feathered hats, crimson sashes,
shell jackets gray as their grave faces.
Done by mid-morning, I amble to the stockade
in search of marketable scenes, portraits of misery
for which morbid Northerners pay gold.

10 a.m.

For unobstructed shots from behind the latrine,
I lug my tripod up the narrow ladder
into one of the fifty-two "pigeon roosts."
August heat intensifies the gagging stench.
A barefoot boy in baggy uniform,
barely tall enough to peek out the nest,
points with his cocked musket at notches
carved in the pine railing,
a private head count of souls dispatched,
of those too close to the prison's dead-line,
a fifteen-yard no man's land,
buffering the stockade wall.
A wink and grin assure me
of the sentinel's accuracy, whether genuine
threat, suicide, or "accidental parole."

Photograph #1:
Trousers dropped, men squat over latrine,
bare buttocks white as eggshells.
Curled at their feet, a dying soldier
succumbs unnoticed.

Noon

From another sentry box I shoot a panorama.

Photographs #2, #3, #4, and #5:
In a twenty-acre stockade,
thirty-three thousand prisoners.
"Shebangs," shelters not big enough,
made of wood scraps, blanket shreds, clothing.
Some men peer from holes in the ground.
Tents disappear into infinity.

1 p.m.

Too late for officers' mess,
I beg food from the bake house.
A niggro offers prisoner fare,
unbolted corn meal, ground
with husks, unfit for consumption,
and beans, weevil-eaten and wormy.

Under a tuft of trees I doze:
a bowl of blackberries and sugar.
Lo, it transfigures into flies and maggots!
To the clip-clop of horseshoes, Captain Wirz sneers,
my toes tied, my body tossed into the dead-wagon.
I awaken, a tremulous aspen leaf.

2 p.m.

With a plug of chaw, I bribe a guard
to escort me through the stockade,
sans camera. He says, *Only iffen you promise
not to pick the flahrs, and keep offen the grass.*

Once inside the pen,
the slaughterhouse-offal-smell suffocates.
Too hot to nap, dime museum skeletons
shuffle, incapable of casting shadows,
their minstrel-black faces begrimed
with pitch-pine smoke from wet stump-roots
they dig and burn to cook raw rations.
Under flimsy rags, skin sags
on protruding bones like walnut bark.

A Dutchman hawks: *Here for meal beer!
Right sour! Well-seasoned with sassafras!*
For five cents, he dips me a pint.
After a sip of the swill, I dump it
over outstretched skeletal hands.

I make it halfway, as far as the creek,
where a mongrel crawls, short of water's edge.
Swarming with maggots, his gangrenous sores
eat to bone. As he tries to die, his eyes,
sun-scorched of tears, iris-out.
I vomit.

3 p.m.

Photograph #6:
Four gabby men washing ragged uniforms
perch on the creek bed like fishermen.
One bathes nude in knee-deep water.

4 p.m.

Wolfish eyes, hollow as spoons, search the horizon
for the tips of the mules' ears
pulling the ration wagon,
the same vehicle used to remove the dead.

Photographs #7 and #8:
A man with a long chinstrap beard
ladles beans and doles out cornbread squares,
stacked like blankets, to squad sergeants.
Prisoners follow just as famished swine
pursue the farmer to the trough.

Taps

Photographs #9 and #10:
Pressed plantation slaves in hats,
shirtsleeves rolled, lower the dead,
shoulder to shoulder, like clothespins in a box.
A bundle of slim, numbered wooden markers
correspond to names recorded in the dead roll.
To placate the darks, upset
over the need to dig another trench,
a Johnnie with a fine fiddle voice

strikes up "Soldier's Joy,"
serenading long after the sun sets.
Requiescat.

———

A fool, I sold the wet plate negatives,
each a Station of some man's *Via Crucis.*
Took me twenty years to hunt each one down,
destroy them, the glass shattering,
the shards, like my nightmares,
pricking, blood on my hands
no soap can wash away.

When I arrived here, I brought one photograph
I shot of Captain Wirz at his hanging
in Capital Prison yard, where the martyrs
of the Lincoln blessing also perished.
The black hood, the tightened noose,
the sprung trap door, the unbroken neck,
the body in eternal gradual strangle.

Every night I remove the hood,
expose the purple face,
hunks of flesh torn by the rope,
eyes popped, tongue swollen,

but the heart,
          the heart.

STAFF SLAUGHTERHOUSE WORKER: JOSIAH CAIN

I witnessed the battlefield surgeon,
too drunk to lop off a leg,
the saw in my hand,
a cannon-rattled Captain ordering me,
a litter bearer, to do the job
before gangrene done him in.

I scouted swarming plains,
black with buffalo, for dude hunters
who took tail, head, or horn,
the carcass left to rot, robbery
not hunting, the prairie white
as snow with bones.

I watched sodbusters scalp
Dakota squaws carrying papooses,
the bodies stiff as straw dolls,
the pelts exchanged for bounty
or displayed on parlor chairs,
memento mori.

———

They call me butcher,
my name the stain on an apron,
blood tinting hands
I scrub every night with lye soap,
fingers and palms raw as the red meat
I slaughter but refuse to eat.

NOVEL READING

```
W. Va. Hospital for the Insane
Name:    Pepper
Admitted: 9 November, 1864
```

I was born property of my mother's master
who raped her in the barn
with the other livestock to increase his fold.
He give me the found name of the whiskey he drank.

Mother toiled in the fields while I crawled underfoot
of the Mistress. She slapped me for gettin' in the way
and for cryin' after my mother. The impression of her
hand stayed with me. When six years old
I knowed I was a slave.

My master's daughter and me played school.
She taught me A, B, C, 'til caught in the loft.
She learned her lesson, and I got a whippin'.

Malinda, master's cook, taught me the rest at night.
I learned writin', numbers, The Book.
When Massa found her pen, ink, and paper,
he flogged her to death. Replacement cost him
$1200 and a mare. To teach me a lesson,
he lopped off part of my writin' finger,
just enough to avoid harm to my resale value.

My new owner didn't know I could read.
He stuffed the bill of sale in my shirt pocket:

Male nigger. Name: Pepper
Age: about 26
Not quite 5 feet eleven and one half inches high
of rather dark-black complexion,

the first finger of the right hand
shorn at the middle knuckle,
machine accident.

After breakfast one mornin', new Massa saddled up,
braggin' he'd whup the Yankees before supper.
New Mistress set an empty table for four years.
One day, Union soldiers runned off everybody,
sold the house for horse spit, and said, *You is free!*
Like an old nag turned loose, I walked away
to the new state, West Virginia. In Charleston,
I holed up in a building with more books
than both my Massas owned slaves. Days later,
they found me hiding in the attic, reading
by candlelight, Voltaire, Dickens, Jefferson.
They called me the black Lincoln.
Arrested for vagrancy, I read in jail.
They called me one crazy Niggro
and sent me to the 'sylum where a white man
dressed as white as an angel slaps me
'cause he stepped in a pile of horse shit I shoud'a seen
and calls me *boy* as I tend garden and animals.

'mancipation!

SEVERE LABOR

```
W. Va. Hospital for the Insane
Name:     Venetia Pearson
Admitted: 14 May, 1870
```

My mother warned me not to marry
a man unless I understood his desires
matched my abilities to fulfill.
So she taught me to sew, bake,
cook, roll tobacco, dance, make soap,
and hit a moving target at 100 yards.
But after three miscarriages,
no darned sock hole, no cobbler,
no dancing around the subject
prevents my man's coldness from settling
on me, blizzard hard and graveyard cold.

———

The midwife, Julia, scowls,
another difficult birth,
coils of cord wrapped 'round the neck
like a rattler,
my bluish baby boy stillborn.
As Julia washes her hands of me,
my man, still without issue,
refuses even a glimpse.
Instead, he gallops off
to clear-burn pasture.

In my arms, I cradle the babe
swaddled in his pall,
a quilting scrap
from a dress my mother wore.
After giving birth to me,

she never knew the color of my eyes
matched the robin-egg bonnet
she bought for sunrise
service, Easter, 1850.

———

In the asylum, a childless place, I
weave blank-faced cornhusk dolls
stuffed with dried hickory leaves.
Their brittle hands clutch
cradleboards made from scraps of sycamore bark
that the colored cook, Rosa, finds
along with herbs and roots she mixes
to concoct potions
for fruitless women like me.
To get with child by the mandrake,
Rosa whispers, her eyes, white haints,
her irises, faint ravens.

LOSS OF LEG

```
W. Va. Hospital for the Insane
Name:    Andrew Sipes
Admitted: 30 May, 1868
```

No longer enemy, not even soldier,
I lie wounded, waiting for the ground
to be regained, my only cover
a uniform rent meaningless by grapeshot
and stained neutral with blood.

I am conscious of the surrounding dead.
Moans from the dying are relieved
by intermittent musketry and cannon.
My lips crack like dried mud.
I sicken at the irony
taste of my blood, am tended to
only by the flies I am unable to shoo.

When night arrives, maybe death
will mistake me for a corpse.
Out of the blackness I hear footsteps.
Lantern light nears.
Someone grabs my hand and I feel
my wedding band stripped off.
I scream.

At dawn, fighting resumes. Minie balls whiz
overhead. Sulfurous clouds of smoke
burn my lungs and sting my eyes
incapable of tears. Maggots worm
through my wounds. I fear
the stretcher bearers, ordered to bring in
only those cases most likely to survive,
will judge me a long shot. Urine stings
the wound I now feel in my leg.

As the shock wears off and pain surrenders
to agony, I black out.

Outside an abandoned slave-hut where I wait
my turn, a door laid on a barrel and a box
serves as an operating table. Some men beg
to be first in line for an amputation.
The surgeon ignores them, his feet swollen,
his hands stained red, his fingernails softened
by the constant bath of water and blood.
Nearby, assistants hone scalpels on shoe soles.

Chloroform drowses. The amputation begins,
a single whack just above the right knee.
My arms break free, reaching upward.
I cry, *Oh, my God!*

My leg is thrown a few feet from the next in line.
A green recruit vomits. A customary prescription
after an amputation is brandy, a favorite
of the surgeon. So there is none.

———

After nine months, I am discharged, a newborn.
The empty space that used to be a pony
frightens my four-year-old. While I drink
away my pension, years pass without touching
my wife. On Decoration Day, after visiting
graves of the war dead, at a church picnic,
when I finish first in the three-legged race,
I refuse to be untied from the preacher
who could not heal like the two-legged Jesus.

From my asylum cot, in dreams,
in the face of enemy fire, I abandon courage
and with two strong legs, run.

SNUFF EATING

```
W. Va. Hospital for the Insane
Name:    Horace Hanion
Admitted: 22 April, 1878
```

I read the ancient Egyptians surrounded their dead
with clothing, jewelry, even furniture, for the afterlife.
They preserved brain, liver, lungs, and stomach
in fancy canning jars. The heart alone remained.

When a Wichita dies, the body rests
atop extinct buffalo hides, feet to East, head to West,
the grave filled with bow, arrows, pottery, and ornaments.
The widow cuts off her hair, braids the locks,
and adorns the spot over her heart.

Pastor Russell predicts the Second Coming
for Good Friday, April 20, 1878.
Lacking tomb or wife, I prepare,
swallowing a compass for direction, coal for warmth,
nails for construction. To record the journey,
I ingest stylus and slate. For indigestion,
I eat several tins of *Tube Rose* snuff.

At three p.m. on Pittsburgh's 6th Street Bridge,
I wait with a throng for the end of the world.
As the sun sets, believers ebb, and I climb
to the tower, closer to God. Midnight arrives.
I remove my clothes. The last of the faithful
abandon me. At dawn, police wave me down
with billy clubs and shrill whistles.

———

As the asylum doctor's fish-cold fingers probe
my abdomen, he asks what I've been eating.

I hem and haw. When I spy the doc's ear horn,
what he calls a stethoscope, used, he says,
to locate, then listen to the heart, it gets me
wondering: Will it go down in one swallow or two?

CARBUNCLE

```
W. Va. Hospital for the Insane
Name:     Amelia Day
Admitted: 27 November, 1864
```

Like a fairy tale it started:

One morning, during the war of '61,
while milking the cow, I hear a moan
coming from the manger,. Sleeping inside,
a young Johnny Reb under floppy cap,
his cherub face besmirched with blood
and battle grime. As I wash the wounds,
he rouses, flinches, asks if I am Mary,
the Mother of Jesus. When I convince him
of my earthly lineage, he proposes
I return with him to Paradise,
Louisiana, his hometown.

He tires of war as I tire of battling Father,
his rejection of all suitors, none fit.
Father wears me down. Wears me
like a locket round his neck,
his pretty possession, his golden girl.
To Ohio, we run away.

I work as a seamstress.
Andrew, a strange man of draft age,
takes a position in a grocery store,
the owner more interested in sales
than the five-dollar bounty on deserters.

When a hideous carbuncle
sprouts on my left cheek,
growing round and red as a war wound,

Andrew avoids touching me.
And as it disappears,
a twin takes its place elsewhere,
my face in continuous plague,
Satan's mock stigmata.

Months go by, no relief.

One morning, I rise, Andrew's side
of the bed, cold as the silver Derringer
I hold, aim, and fire at my reflection
in the vanity mirror.
Throughout town, hammer in hand,
I hunt down, smash every looking glass,
my horrid image reflected over and over
at my feet, looking up at me, haunting.

———

In my asylum room, drop cloths shroud
reflective surfaces. Like the target
of an execution, the doctor blindfolds me.
At night, the colored cook, Rosa,
reads to me from the Bible,
bringing to mind a childhood memory:

Once, at bedtime, before reading Grimm,
Father held up Mother's sterling hand mirror
and asked me what I saw. I shrugged.
He answered for me, *Beauty*.
Then he held it under my nose,
asking if I could see my breath
misted on the glass. I nodded.
Again, he held the glass before me.
Now what do you see?
His eyes narrowed

as though the oil lamp burned low.
Nothing, I whispered.
I remember his smile,
like a grateful schoolmaster,
when he whispered back,
Such is Beauty.

STAFF SAWMILL WORKER: ARBY PERSINGER

Before steam, I was better off.
As a pitman, standing in the hole
below the log, I pulled the saw
back-and-forth, the teeth biting
through cypress and pine, a shower
of sawdust sprinkling me,
blessings from the Holy Carpenter.

In a modern steam-sawmill in Lookout,
Pennsylvania, steam-powered machines
slab, saw up, shove out the mill
and stack the timber.
All I do is sweat for twelve hours,
feeding the beast raw logs
for a dollar fifty a day.

The morning the boiler explodes,
I figure Jesus come again
on a scalding cloud of steam,
hell-bent for The Rapture.
But I ain't taken to paradise.

I don't even die.

After removing the facial bandages,
Doc's face sours—*Boy, be glad you're alive.*
When I look in the shaving mirror,
I shudder, my features disfigured,
mottled with browns, pinks, reds,
a rotting log dotted by lichen.

No woman gives me the once-over twice,
so I move back to Weston, West Virginia,
grow a beard, and find work
at the new asylum where I blend in.

One day, a patient, a young lady
with a carbuncle-ravaged face,
begs turpentine to clean oil brushes.
Her eyes do not avert
when she asks me to sit
for a portrait. I refuse.
Why? she asks. But I turn away.
Grabbing my dusty elbow sleeve,
she explains she meant no disrespect.

For weeks, under a sycamore, she paints
me while I eat lunch. Like a carpenter
eyeing hewn timber, she studies
my features, her brush dobbing
gobs of paint, creating an image
she declines to reveal 'til finished.

At the mill one evening, closing time,
she unveils the painting, her eyes bright
as fresh varnish, her lips a cherry veneer.
As I gaze at the portrait of horror,
she asks, *What do you see?*
I shrug,
hand back the monstrosity.
When I leave this place, she says,
I am taking your beauty with me.

Beauty?
Just lunatic ramblings,
I tell myself, rising from my cot
at midnight to look at my shaved face
again in the mirror
I bought,
first one since the accident.

HARD STUDY

```
W. Va. Hospital for the Insane
Name:     Gus Carter
Admitted: 17 September, 1866
```

At first, crowds cheered, pretty girls waved
flags, the rich picnicked on cold chicken
on knolls overlooking battlefields.
We would teach the Blue Bellies a lesson.
But come winter, I huddled from icy blasts
behind a five-foot-high wall of dead soldiers.

After the war, I returned
to college to continue my study of civilization
from professors, jack-a-dandies
who ain't never...

Science

As a farm boy familiar with planting,
my superiors ordered a fruitless chore.
On hands and knees I buried
sub-terra explosive shells
inches below a dirt road.
Then in the bushes I hid, a witness
to the efficiency of modern war.
When Union Calvary charged,
the detonations dismembered
bodies with the bloodlust of Ares.
By God, I am familiar with harvest, too.

Foreign Language

In '61, on a road somewhere south
of Manassas, I met a soldier.
Like a rabid coonhound,
he feared neither man nor god.

A-fightin', a-killin', five weeks
stiddy, n-a-rthin' to eat 'cept
a peck of sour-green apples
and a few years of green cawn.
But I know whar the grapes
of wrath is stored. Thar in the
midguts of Southern boys
that Union artillery opened
up tin cans on and stuffed
their bread baskets
full of grapeshot.

Literature

After a skirmish at Bull Pasture,
in the statue-stiff hand of a boy
soldier, I found his letter home:

My Dearest Beloved Mother,

Do not fret over me. I thrive
on fatback-biscuits and creek water.
Tonight, before battle,
I take comfort in knowing you love me.

I know Father disapproves of my decision
to fight with Yankees,
but you taught me from the Book
that God created all in His image.
Like the prodigal, I hope to return
to Father's loving embrace.

Come dawn, I carry our regiment colors.
Not a stitch will touch ground.
I swear.
But I confess I am afraid
I may lose courage

shook by the knell of cannon,
frightened by the fury of musket fire
and the edge of the bayonet.

So I let the words of Our Lord echo:
Let not your heart be troubled...
For if strangers tuck me under
the corner-sod of some forgotten battlefield,
do not seek me beneath buckthorn and briar,
for...*in my Father's house
are many mansions.*

History

The night before battle, sniper rounds
whizzed like shooting stars,
and sporadic cannons interrupted
last letters home, cat naps,
and dreams of Sunday
breakfast, pone and bacon.
Me, I dreamed of shoes.

Before dawn, September 17, 1862,
at support arms, we hid in a 30-acre cornfield.
A pall of fog prevented accurate artillery.
As the Blues advanced, our muskets fired,
the smoke mixing with sweat,
painting a greasy black stain over our faces
like the sin of Cain.
In the thundercloud of battle,
I wandered firing point blank at other phantoms
I could recognize
neither as friend nor foe.

When the sun reflected, flashed
off our bayonets above the green stalks,
betraying our position, Federal cannonades

propelled twelve-pound shells.
In minutes, harvest arrived
quicker than the autumn scythe.

The cornfield changed hands four times.

Under an indifferent sun, colored blood-red
by red clay and the haze of ten thousand rounds,
men dropped like seed strewn amongst rock,
thorn, and thistle along a silent farm creek,
Antietem.

Mathematics

Before the war, his daddy
give my cousin, Pat Bowden,
his forty birthright acres,
where his seventeen-year-old wife,
Lucy, waited for him in the eight-
room farmhouse he built for her
and six planned youngins.

When I visited her after the war,
her hair in a bun under a crepe bonnet,
her face shrouded by a weeping veil,
I climbed three wooden porch steps
and returned his personal effects:
one watch chain made from Lucy's hair,
(the gold watch, he bartered for food),
one wedding band, forged from plantation
candelabra silver melted down before the war,
and one hand-carved cross of Cypress,
the tree of mourning,
the wood of coffins, sacred,
but only to the god of the underworld.

———

Returning to college, in the rear of a classroom,
my back against the wall, I study my perimeter.
A flicker of lightning mutates to the flash of muskets,
a peal of thunder to cannon fire.
As the professor babbles next to the flag stand,
the colors vulnerable, I spy a weakness in his flank
and charge. After classmates pry me from him,
he snivels in the corner, defeated,
his smarts of no use.

The asylum doctor says
my mind misfires like a defective musket
because I have grown a soldier's heart.
When I grab his arm a little too tight
and beg him to pluck it out
like a dud bullet pulled from a rifle barrel,
he shouts for reinforcements.
As orderlies straightjacket me,
the doctor removes his pince-nez and stares at me
like I don't know nothin'.

WOMEN TROUBLE

```
W. Va. Hospital for the Insane
Name:    Emily Besong
Admitted: 27 August, 1884
```

At quilting bees, Emily watches the chore-
callused hands of farm women transform
into butterflies, fluttering, delicate as stitches
connecting lives together like love letters
she wishes she could write.

In secret, Emily inhales their fragrances,
defined by spices of the season:
spring mint, fennel used in herbal tea
to enhance breast milk, Jamaican allspice
for cooking wild game, holiday flavorings
like nutmeg, cinnamon, and ginger,
the piquant flavor of cloves,
and turmeric for a batch of winter butter.

Caring for her best friend, Anna,
after she breaks a leg gentling a new plow horse,
Emily sits on the edge of the tub,
the bath water infused with thyme
and tosses in its two-lipped, pale rose flowers
like pennies into a wishing well.

They bob and kiss Anne's body, imparting
a subtle woodsy flavor to her pink skin.
To the Greeks, Anna says, *thyme symbolized
courage. Ladies embroidered sprigs
on the battle scarves of their knights.*

As she sponges water onto Anna's back
and watches dark ringlets of hair curl
like garden tendrils, Emily adds,

Egyptians used thyme to preserve the body,
to assure passage to another life.

At choir practice, women crack open
song books like breakfast biscuits.
Emily watches Anna's tongue lick her
fingertips to turn pages. As she sings,
her mouth opens, round and receptive
as canning jars brimmed with honey.
Her throat quavers,
her neck the color of churned cream.
And through her cotton tea bodice,
as the notes undulate, Emily watches
the rise and fall of Anna's nipples.
The wanderlust of her fancies arrest
at the start of *Amazing Grace,*
leaving Emily to ponder
how God can save a wretch like her.

For a church social, in Anna's kitchen,
Emily helps bake sugary treats,
Kisses and Secrets.

Beat the white of six eggs to a stiff froth.
Anna twirls the whisk in the wooden bowl,
rattling like a stick on a picket fence
or the thrumming of a heart-shaped lyre.
Add powdered sugar and juice of an orange.
Anna crushes and twists the orange
on the reamer, and the juice flows.
Inhaling the dusty powdered sugar,
Emily savors the explosion of sweetness
on the back of her tongue
Butter baking sheet.
After Emily spreads butter barehanded
over the baking sheet, Anna wipes off

each of her fingers with her apron.
Dollop thick dough and bake.
By the warm oven Anna and Emily prepare
single poem verses on threaded paper
to be wrapped 'round the finished cookies.
Emily's hand shakes while penning
the words of Sappho:
"My lips are stricken to silence;
a subtle flame burns beneath my skin."

After Anna removes the cookies,
she blows one cool and offers it
like a sacred wafer of manna.
Emily accepts the offering,
and her wet lips glide across Anna's fingers.
As the cookie dissolves like a dream,
Emily clutches Anna's apron, pulls
her close, and kisses her on the mouth.

REMORSE

```
W. Va. Hospital for the Insane
Name:    Gilbert McCorkle
Admitted: 6 April, 1886
```

I never saw a face, only a target,
moving cautious like a stag

off guard for a trigger-second,
the crack
      of the shot,
            muffled,

a shirt wrapped 'round the barrel,

           unnoticed
at first,
      then chaos. Then I, too,

departed.

Silhouettes in the cross-hairs, haunted,
still yearning to be homeward bound,
arguing the bushel-price of corn,
assisting in the birth of a calf.

———

As for man, his days are as grass...
Grandson runs across the asylum meadow;
a flopping fish dangles from his line.
for the wind passes over it and it is gone...
As my daughter nurses her third,
my wife's hair waves in the breeze
like the promise of winter wheat.
and the place thereof shall know it no more.

HEREDITARY PREDISPOSITION

    W. Va. Hospital for the Insane
    Name: Zella Kerns
    Admitted: 11 October, 1887

Dad keeps two books on his office desk,
the Bible and Spinoza's *Ethics*.
Pressed between the two,
a stack of suicide notes, collected
over thirty years as coroner.

One day, in my youth, I read the notes:

Case #1857-016

Martha,
I can no longer hide our destitution.
In the bank panic, I lost everything
of value I wanted
to bequeath the children:
cattle, horses, carriages,
the gristmill, acreage
by the lake where I taught them
to swim, to keep their heads
above water.

Creditors will demand an accounting,
will find the inventory short
two 50 lb. sacks of grain,
for the weight,
to prevent faintheartedness.
If they squawk,
tell them to go jump in the lake!

Case #1860-009

You snake!
Through my veins, the poison
of your adulterous lies radiates,
paralyzes my heart.
But never too late to let blood.
Your straight razor will do,
will glide like a violin bow
across my wrists,
the final note, B-flat minor,
the feeling I get
when I am all alone.

Case #1866-031

Father,
Cob jobs! Sloppy work!
Not ever level enough.
My carpentry always suspect.
You crucified me to your trade,
me, a splinter in your finger
you never could extract.

As you perch at your county fair
blue-ribbon-perfect dinner table,
the dust of saws, planes, and bores
falling from your beard, flecking
your pumpernickel and hogget
like bitter herbs, chew on this:
when you cut me down,
sever the limb as well.
Build me a box. Strike the dowels
with a dead-blow mallet
to minimize damage
to the soft yielding flesh

of your precious pinewood.
And make it level enough
to keep these bones
from rattlin'.

One note in particular,
the handwriting familiar:
the bellies of the p's and b's exposed;
the legs of the f's, g's, and y's dangling
like downed telegraph wires;
the necks of h's, k's, and l's,
thin, eyeless needles.

The woman doesn't explain, expresses sorrow
for the pain, if any, caused her husband
for leaving a daughter, too young
to understand, the note
ending, long before the page bottoms out
into a blemish of ink from a leaky nib,
the name *Adele,* drowned.

———

Yesterday, Dad visits, brings the Bible
and *Ethics.* I choose Spinoza.
Suicide can never be a rational choice,
he reads, stressing key words as if I am deaf,
but always results from being overcome
by external causes.

The dear man will want to understand
my last testament. Perhaps he will
comfort himself with Proverbs:
Each heart knows its own joy,
and no one else can share its bitterness.

Perhaps he will marry my note with mother's.
Perhaps he will burn them all in the fireplace
and warm himself in the mystery,
like a good book.

When they think I am out of danger,
they let me roam the asylum,
so while the light lingers,
I search the grounds for an accessible limb,
one stronger than I,
beyond the reach of memory
or meaning.

RELIGIOUS EXCITEMENT

W. Va. Hospital for the Insane
Name: Rev. Msgr. Brian O'Donnell
Admitted: 9 October, 1888

Through cathedral stained glass,
I stare at the newly erected phallus
to honor a Revolutionary god,
Washington, *Pater patriae,*
the golden calf-boy of the masses.
Me, I satisfy my appetites
at the altar of a carnal god.

The echo of pubescent choir boys
seduces like the whispers of impurity
I coax from penitent lambs in the confessional.
Details of their self-abuse flush my face
like sacramental wine
while my cassock-cloaked ardor
hardens as I peer through the honey-
comb of confessional screen,
beckoning them closer, closer, closer,
their dewy breaths blood-warm on my cheek.

After daily Mass, I dim the sacristy gas light.
Januis clausis, behind closed doors,
an altar boy assists, removes my vestments.
Tiny delicate hands, not yet coarse
from farmhand chores,
flutter over my body like a sculptor,
whittling the clay of new creation.

Like the layered veils of Salome,
he slips off chasuble, stole, and maniple,
armor of my purity, chastity, concupiscence.

To remove the cincture, his arms hug
my waist. Fingers fumble to untie the knot
I tied tighter than a hangman's noose.
After removing the last vestments,
alb and amice, he removes my trousers.

When rumors turn to roars,
(*Damnant quod non intelligent:*
They condemn what they don't understand.)
I appeal to the Bishop.
We think, *uno animo,* with one mind,
he and I, two adjacent beads
on the same rosary.
Over a bottle of amontillado,
when I remind his Excellency
of his own *mea culpa* in this area,
(*Similis simili gaudet:*
Like takes pleasure in like.)
he licks his fat purple lips, chuckles,
and says, *In vino veritas.*

When I am transferred to Weston,
West Virginia, the carriage drops me off
at an asylum. The administrator greets me
with a terse, unsigned note in the Bishop's hand:
Quos deus vult perdere prius dementat:
Those whom a god wishes to destroy,
he first drives mad.

———

Strolling the grounds this autumn,
I enjoy the slow striptease of sycamores,
first leaves, then bark, to bare white flesh.
On the other side of the wrought iron fence,

down by the river, boys, bright as dandelions,
play, wrestle with each other.
Naturam expellas furca tamen usque recurret:
Though you drive nature out with a pitchfork,
she will keep coming back.

STAFF COOK: ROSA

Before freedom, I was born
Master's child,
but he never paid me no mind
except to say, *One day, you'll be*
worth a thousand dollars to me.

In the Great House, Mama cooked.
My younger sister collected firewood,
toted water, and ground corn.
Me, I picked, cleaned, cut vegetables
from the slave garden I tilled, sowed, weeded.
Mama told me my whole hands be green,
so she learned me the secret of 'erbs:
goatweed for the influenza,
black cohosh for womanly cramps,
carenco leaves for arthritis,
arrowhead for teething babies.
She also learned me the poisons:
mandrake, castor beans, lobelia
when properly used.

The older I grew, the more I felt
Master's eyes sprouting all over me.
In our room one winter, skullduggery.
Mama, pretending sleep, watched
Master size up her two daughters,
rousing his choice. He crooked
a finger to follow. In Mistress's kitchen,
in a voice I never heard from him,
he told me to take off my clothes;
he wanted to pick black cotton.
I said, *No.*
He switched me with a hickory.
So I became his *Yes, suh* woman.

On the hard wood floor he slaved
to the body he said he owned.

After weeks of the same,
my blood no longer flowed.
Mama said Master's seed
rooted and commenced to grow.
But de Lo'd fixed a way, she said.
We's can weed yo' garden
wit' a potion of juniper berry
an' slippery elm ba'k.
But I tell her, *No. My child be born*
and one day be free.

Sister played, guessing what name
Mistress gonna give the new slave.
When Master told me the stork
delivered white babies and slaves
hatched from buzzards' eggs,
my baby kicked.

I sewed scraps of agreeable-soft flour sack
Mama snitched for my baby's pantalets.
One night, under a full moon,
while I fed the mules, the animals jittered.
A hinny brayed. A foal kicked me.

On straw I birthed.

In fallow ground by fluttering candle
light, we buried a female.
She pretty as a gingerbread doll,
and she free.
Me, childless mother, moaned
heartsick. Fearing the Master
would awaken and hear me calling

on the Maker, Mama hushed me.
A cock crowed.

Rain clouds shrouded the moon,
draping the Great Heaven in mourning.
Wind swished like an empty rattle
through the field, a slumbery crib
quilt of black cotton.

When Master seen I lost his property,
he bullwhipped me, and Mama, too.
Her wounds never healed. In a fever
no remedy she knew could cure,
she passed. Next morning, Master demanded breakfast
be served by me, the new cook. In Mama's apron,
I schemed my own recipe of 'erbs.
Over a month's time, Master took to bed.

At his funeral, I cried my apron limp.
But Mistress stared at me
like she could read my dark heart.
She threw out all of Mama's 'erbs,
made my youngest sister the cook,
and chained me with the smith's anvil,
Tank! Deling-ding! Tank! Deling-ding!
'Round my feet iron shackles echoed,
clanging wherever I goed.
She said, *We'll see how you take
to picking cotton.*

Before dawn the ram horn blew.
'Round my neck hung an empty sack.
At row's end a two-barrel-basket
waited, shy a hundred and fifty pounds.
Stooped, I picked, hands quick
as ground birds sifting through bush.

I was scared of snapping
a branch from the stalk,
as cotton won't bloom on one broken,
and the Overseer didn't miss a twig.

As long as we could see, we stayed in the field.
When the order came to stop,
I toted my basket to the gin-house.
Short twenty pounds, I got twenty
lashes. Afterwards, while feeding the mules,
I swore to the Book I gonna run away.

Under moonlight in the field,
one of Mistress's chattel scratched me a map
in earth to a river called Ohio.
Follow the drinking gourd,
he whispered and pointed to the dipper
a-pointin' to the North Star.
He showed me signs to a conductor,
General Tubman, a colored woman
who gonna take me underground
on the train to Freedom...
Freedom...where I know
what it's like to own my own body.

Next night, to muffle the noise, I wrapped
my chains in burlap. As Mama slept,
I kissed her goodbye.
I took a poke of salted pork,
cornbread, beans, and taters.
Through field and fence and wood, I ran
'til dawn when I stopped and rested my head
on moss, but the ground, it started a-tremblin',
riders thundering like a herd of iron horses,
bloodhounds baying, *Owoo, ow, ow!*
That raised me like Lazarus.

Hunters fired bird shot so's not to damage
me, 'cause there was no reward if they killed
or crippled Mistress's straying property.
The shooting and the howling started
the Whitney plantation slaves a-singin',
Wade in the water. Wade in the water,
chil'. God's gonna trouble the water.
So I ran through the creek.
I ran fast 'til the sound
of them hounds and them slaves died.

By day I hid in hollow trees,
in corn shocks, caves, and swamps.
By night I read the sky, following
the North Star like a moth
follows the moon. For something to eat,
I trapped possum and ember-roasted bullfrogs.
At a crossroad, a reward poster
I couldn't read, excepting the black figures,
$200, big as swamp leeches
I singed off my legs and feet.

Mama used to frighten me as a little tyke
about the evil ghost of ol' Patty Cannon,
who ketched runaways
and sold them back to slavery,
but I was more feared of live people
than dead ones.

As rain poured, thunderbolts lit up
a black groomsman,
a hitching post white men used
that pointed to a Friend's house
where they removed my chains.
I spent the night covered by a quilt
with sewn pictures to the next station.

When slave hunters roused my savior
Quakers, I escaped to their cellar tunnel.
I crawled, wondering how far I could go
swallowed by the earth without suffocating.
Muddy, I arrived at the river's swollen edge
and waded into terrible cold water.
My legs numbed. In the swift current,
I drifted like a log, not knowing
what waited 'round the river bend:
waterfall, hounds, or freedom.

———

On a Mennonite farm, I earn my keep,
cooking, sewing, growing 'erbs.
After meals, I tote scraps to slop the hogs.
Marcus, a farmhand, another runaway,
shadows me at a distance, his grin
beaming like a full moon.
One day, I ask him, *You sweet on one of the sows?*
He smiles, takes my slop bucket,
and sets it upside down for me to sit on.
Kneeling in front of me, he takes my hand,
gentle as a nesting sparrow. *Rosa,*
he says, *I believe I have something you need.*
His eyes, brown chestnuts, warm
more than my hand. I say,
I have everything worth havin'.
But his eyes never stray.
How 'bout a man?
I laugh, say, *Mama learned me 'bout men.*
She told me men are like rivers;
they don't change much.
He frowned, looking more downhearted
than a drowning man.

Course, I say, *Mama also learned me
how to swim.*

Evenings in the barn loft,
Marcus teaches me to read and write.
He talks about his time as a slave
on a tobacco plantation,
how, as a child, he hid from the overseer
in the curing barn, crouching, still as a toad,
staring up at the broad leaves suspended
from rafters, browning into wings
he imagined would fly him to freedom.
When Marcus grew old enough to harvest,
a gray-haired Negro guided his hand,
learning him to snap leaves off proper at the stem.
By day's end, tobacco gum glued his fingers
together like a caterpillar's cocoon.
He thought he would turn into a butterfly.
But the only flying he ever done was
outracing the slave catcher's hounds.

During the freedom war,
Marcus joins the 5th US Colored Cavalry.
Before he leaves, he promises, upon return,
to marry me if I'll have him. I tell him,
You be the only thing worth havin'.

His letters bring comfort,
bright as lanterns in a barn at midnight.
In October '64, the letters stop.
A month later, a white Union officer
trots onto the farm, walks
his chestnut Morgan toward me
after Mr. Shetler points to me in the garden.
As his animal grazes, he fumbles, hat in hand,

describes the heroic efforts of a black
soldier at the Battle of Saltville.
He asks forgiveness, for he brought no memento,
the body buried in a mass grave.

When he leaves, hours remain 'til sunset;
I have time to finish harvesting
the last root crops: beets, carrots, parsnips.
Tomorrow I will rake plant debris and fall-till the soil,
preparing the garden for the approach of winter.

OPIUM HABIT

```
W. Va. Hospital for the Insane
Name:     Alice Lloyd
Admitted: 3 November, 1865
```

14 February, 1865

Alas, my time no longer my own. Henry seems fit enough. Only six weeks after his medical discharge and it waxes within me. To keep the nausea and vomiting at bay I take opium tablets the Army surgeon gave Henry for his arm trampled by a cavalry horse.

29 March, 1865

Morning sickness gone. But I do not feel square. Henry's mother suspects my mettle. Henry still cannot obtain suitable employment. Pills gone.

10 April, 1865

I visit Mrs. Corbin, her husband's hand crushed in a mining accident. Stubborn as a seam of anthracite, he neither takes doctor's advice, nor medicine. In the carpetbag I use to carry over a pot roast, I kidnap his bottle of laudanum.

14 April, 1865

The president murdered! Grief beyond bearing! Laudanum gone.

2 May, 1865

For a moment, I think the druggist spies me. But while I slide a bottle of *Godfrey's Cordial* into my bustle, it is not my hands that catch his eye.

9 May, 1865

Henry leaves, searching for work in Grafton. On pretense of a delivery, the druggist calls. The nerve! Wanting to know if he might "ponder my belly in the state of nature." No! I tell him to keep the morphine tablets he offers. His apologies effusive, the pillbox shoved into his pants pocket, smug as a revolver.

11 May, 1865

In the back room, the druggist leers at my edematous abdomen. When his breathing labors, I cover up. In any case, he is almost a doctor. Only three pills.

13 May, 1865

Breasts. Six pills.

17 May, 1865

On the train ride to Buckhannon, he assures discretion. Afterwards, in the motel...I pray Henry never finds out.

23 June, 1865

In church, for an hour, the preacher anatomizes the evils of adultery. His eyes loiter like a fly's, my bosom, plentiful as whortleberries. In the pew, I fidget, his ogle, hot as any brand. Afterwards, his mule-nosed wife interrogates.

4 July, 1865

On straw in his friend's barn, like pestle in mortar, he grinds, prickles, explodes inside me like a glass firecracker.

30 August, 1865

Delivery. The midwife never saw one so disagreeable.

29 September, 1865

I demand to know why he ignores me. When I press him, he says his wife...wife...wife. To avoid any "appearance of impropriety," he cannot...*will* not give me anymore pills. When I threaten to tell his wife, wife, wife, he glowers, smirks as a customer passes, then fills an unlabelled amber bottle with tonic. I do not budge until he fills two more.

7 October, 1865

My man settles for factory work out of town. The colicky waif wails like a mewing, puking bobcat. Nothing quiets it, except a dose of my tonic.

1 November, 1865

Found this morning, cold as a quarter-moon, the body. In the milking-rocker, I brood. The doctor shrugs, telegrams husband.

2 November, 1865

At the wake, proper as any gentleman, he offers condolences. At the coffin, tiny as a hatbox, he pauses, leans in, whispers, his breath sickly-sweet as penny candy, his voice cozy, "You can always bear another."

BAD COMPANY

W. Va. Hospital for the Insane
Name: Patrick Henderson
Admitted: 24 July, 1883

I have known Patrick Henderson since birth.
To ease delivery, I pilfered church-bell-rope
from the ringer and tied it 'round his mother's waist.
But cursed the child born on Thursday: Inclined to thieving!

At Baptism, the priest never drove the Devil out,
for the babe refused to cry, despite my pinches.
At First Communion, a raven perched on the rail,
as sure an omen as the shadow of a lynched murderer.

As his schoolmistress, I spared no rod,
birching the boy every day, having my fill
of his shenanigans, playing the fox, disrupting class
like the smell of Mrs. Bane's blackberry cobbler.

The Army shaved his head, drummed him out
to the tune of a *Rogue's March,* brow branded:
"BC," Bad Character. Caught stealing money
from a wounded comrade. On the battlefield!

Outside the barbershop, like a hotel fern, the dastard squats,
growing more odorous and hairier than necessary.
When drunk, he preaches temperance to saloon whores
on the Sabbath for nickels and slugs.

The night we convince a judge to sign papers,
we bind him, baptize him in a horse trough,
and hand him over. The asylum doctor rebukes us.
Us! Saying he ain't never seen such bad company!

STAFF SUPERINTENDENT: DR. R.T. FERGUSON

Esteemed Members of the Board of Directors,

As the Board considers these allegations, I remind you of the unique nature of our patients, their tendency to fantasize, to exaggerate the true nature of relationships, especially with staff quartered here, like myself along with my five children. (As an aside, my beloved wife fulfills all my carnal necessities.)

Each preceding administration faced like charges. Although I taught that woman, Miss Marcum, to waltz, as part of a bona fide patient therapy to improve her disposition, her youth and beauty escaped my professional scrutiny. Her pregnancy, terminated by herbal abortifacients, of which I am determined to find the source, grieves me more than these malicious charges.

Cordially,
Superintendent, Dr. R. T. Ferguson

———

At night, like a horned screamer, he appears
outside my door, keys rattling like bones
of decomposed prey. Silent as shadow,
he creeps to my bed. Overpowering,
his toilet water nauseates. Cold fingers
graze my face, worm their way down
beneath my gown, and clutch
me, a modest field mouse.

I turn my face away from the sound
of his zipper, cleaving, the smell
of his fusty breath as he pants.
When he kisses my mouth,
I taste the fowl he shot that afternoon
and gorged at supper.

Before leaving, he whispers, *Miss Marcum,*
my little chickabiddy, not a peep.

When my flow ceases, I befriend
Rosa, the conjuring cook.
She mashes pennyroyal, catnip,
and juniper berries into a blood-red potion,
and assures me my stream will return.
In exchange, I swear secrecy.
That night, pains worse than Eve's curse
leave me void of maternity.

———

Gentleman of the Board,

    I am grateful for the board members' Solomonic wisdom.
Your verdict, "not guilty," redeems me, a man of fine timber, a cedar
of Lebanon. In the future, I look forward to similar insight when
investigating current charges made by my secretary, her grief over
the loss of husband understandable, reason enough for hysterical
fabrications.

        As ever,
        Superintendent, R. T. Ferguson

———

In a cradle Rosa fashioned from cedar scraps,
my baby sleeps on a mat of straw.
The babe cut her finger on a fugitive nail.
Funny thing, after sewing up the wound,
Rosa apologized, leaving me muddled,
saying, *Sometimes, child, the cure I conjure,*
like a well-aimed dueling pistol, backfires,
the ball striking the heart of the unintended.

CONFINEMENT

> W. Va. Hospital for the Insane
> Name: Ben Lanternman
> Admitted: 12 July, 1885

Not until I fancy a glass of udder-warm milk
do I consider desertion.
One evening, after watering the horses,
I wander the road toward the enemy.
At each farmhouse, I knock,
but days earlier Confederates commandeered
everything drinkable or edible.
As I amble further south, I long for home,
for Mother in Tennessee.

A scouting party startles my reverie. I ask,
Who are you? A pimple-faced captain
spits a wad of chaw at my feet, says,
The enemy.
I explain my desire to see Mother,
my sympathy toward the Rebels,
my hankering for milk.

Captain grins. The head scout questions:
How your pickets stationed?
How strong your position?
How armed?
As the sun sets, I peach.
Then, Captain asks to see my revolver.
After handing it over, he cocks it, aims,
and orders me to hand over belt and saber.

At camp, they tie me to the chuck wagon,
where Reb soldiers pluck my whiskers.
One pisses in a tin cup
and offers it to me like a glass of warm milk.

Dawn, my company attacks.
A shell splinters the wagon. Dazed, I run,
follow two deserting Confederate soldiers
into an abandoned coal mine.
In the throat of the cave, we listen
to the battle until a shell explodes,
sealing us inside.

By match light, we find an oil lantern.
During the collapse, one of them,
Tom Obney, fractured a leg,
the fibula breaking skin, protruding
like a pope's nose.

Day eight:
Gangrene, the maggoty skunk of death.
Obney hallucinates.
I hold him. He enters the heavenly country
calling me Pa. Afterwards,
John Ewing rifles the warm body
for provisions.

Day ten:
Canteen water and field rations gone.
I watch Ewing cut off Obney's buttocks
and eat it as he dances around,
brandishing his bowie.

Day thirteen:
Oil scarce. Air foul.
Alone with the dead.
In self-defense, I had to
strangle the madman, Obney.
Several bites perforate his left foot.
Full, sleepy, I wait for death.

———

From the asylum, not even nightmares escape:

The 13th. 3:00 p.m.
The firing party of twelve comrades
marches to within six paces of me,
in their arms, Sharp's breech-loading rifles.

A stiff-necked chaplain proposes paradise.
I get a noseful
of the holy scent of pine,
the coffin beside me without inscription.
Winds, dry as tumbleweeds, howl.
As I listen to four buglers play taps,
I have no spit to wet my lips.

The Provost reads the final order
of execution. Words brand me:
deserter, traitor, cannibal.
After the blindfold, I confess
my last testament,
Boys, may God forgive us all.

Too shaky to stand, I squat on coffin's rim,
the sudden volley, like a murder of crows taking flight.
For a moment I pose, quiver, and fall
into the box. Wounds bloom.
Still alive. A reserve completes the duty.
Above my left eyebrow,
the bullet enters my brain.
Hammer meets nail.
Dirt ratatats the wooden roof.

I rise

from my cot, gasping for breath,
heart war-drumming in the soldier's ward.

On the nightstand, my Medal of Honor,
for gallantry in pursuit of the enemy.
Even after twenty-two years the base metal gleams,
of habit, my fingers rubbing
the relief of Minerva,
goddess of wisdom and war,
the fine lines of distinction
worn to blur.

SMALLPOX

```
W. Va. Hospital for the Insane
Name:    Dr. Woodrow Harper
Admitted: 18 November, 1864
```

As I watch ragged retreating soldiers
shoot farm animals and dump them
into ponds Yankees depend on for drinking,
I recall reading how native tribes in Aptos
gave Spaniards gifts of fresh-cut flowers
wrapped in leaves of poison oak,
and a reverie overshadows my soul:
What if Yankee soldiers warmed themselves
with blankets contaminated with smallpox?

From hospitals, I reap a deadly harvest.
I transport them myself to Baltimore
where I ship the "donations" by rail
to the Union depot outside Gettysburg.

> Lincoln meets with his generals and
> stays the night in a tent near Gettysburg,
> wanting to sleep with the multitude
> of soldiers, anonymous as the stars.
> To wrap Lincoln's lanky frame,
> a corporal supplies several blankets,
> a new shipment from
> *The only crate of donations not stolen*
> *by Rebel train robbers, sir.*

How could I know Confederates would attack
the train, steal the blankets, distribute them
to the Charleston Orphan House?

> On the train, Lincoln's doctor monitors
> the dizziness, but the president insists

on delivering a speech
at a new-begotten battlefield.
The statesman scribbles a few notes,
using his stovepipe hat as a desk.

While Lincoln speaks, miles away,
I doctor the youngest orphans myself.
Four-year-old Shawn says he sees the Lord
walking toward him with a red Irish Setter.
When I tell him to run toward the dog,
I feel his heart explode like a string of firecrackers,
and then it stops.

       Upon returning to the White House,
       Lincoln develops a scarlet, blister-like rash.
       Diagnosis: smallpox.
       Under quarantine for three weeks,
       while rumors spread of a dying leader,
       he jokes: *For once in my life as president,*
       I find myself in a position
       to give everybody something!

       ———

On good days, like today, I assist
the asylum doctor, performing an autopsy
on the corpse of a soldier, a Medal of Honor
recipient, who hung himself.
While he studies the ligature marks, we talk
philosophy: Darwin, struggle, adaptation,
how the strongest survive.

When the doctor removes the brain
and plops it into a jar of formaldehyde,
he says, *War has changed us.*

I shake my head, say, *No,*
we have changed war,
and reach for the rib shears
to release the heart.

MARRIAGE OF SON

```
       W. Va. Hospital for the Insane
       Name:    Claudia Phillips
       Admitted: 14 February, 1867
```

There's a powerful connection 'twixt us.
I almost died birthing my only child, Nathan,
me, a ghost my mama conjured back to life
with Satan's apple and the Lord's Prayer.
When he was nine, he got St. Anthony's Fire
from bad rye grain. He moaned as his body burned
like a brimstone sermon from Reverend Simms.
But, like Lazarus, I doctored him back from the pit.

For three years while my husband fought the Yanks,
I watched Nathan's limbs grow like the oak,
and when the black-bordered telegram arrived,
I took shelter under those broad boughs.
At eighteen, Nathan became the man of my house.
For a year he slept on the empty side of my bed
but stopped after meeting that apple-cheeked
war orphan, Sarah, a pesky snipe who loved
to nest in his branches. That's when I cast off
my widow's weeds. What I done, it's in the Bible:
Genesis 19:23-36, Lot's daughters.

On my fourteenth day, I spotted the signs,
so that night, after shooing Sarah away, I got out
the shine and liquored up Nathan. While he dozed
in his bed, I rouged my cheeks, sprayed Lilac
Imperial toilet water, and let down my hair.
Before rousing him, I trimmed the lamp wick.
By God, my birthright would remain mine.

I was going on two months when Nathan told me
that on Sunday their wedding banns would be called.
That evening I heard the lovebirds in the barn,
so me and my old man's Colt Walker went snipe hunting.
Through the broken window I spied her, naked,
her hips, a wide tree trunk, good for fruitful bearing.
When a hoot owl spooked me, the gun fired
astray, but my second shot hit the heifer's eye.
But only after I heard Nathan's dying moan,
did I feel it, the burn, St. Anthony's Fire,
God's eternal punishment.

By the light of a harvest moon, I planted.

———

After I started showing, I set the church ablaze.
To a sleepy-eyed judge, the sheriff explained
how my only son eloped for greener pastures.
He signed the papers quicker than striking a match,
sending me to the lunatic asylum in Weston.

There, I almost died birthing my second son.

FIGHTING FIRE

W. Va. Hospital for the Insane
Name: William Eliot
Admitted: 8 October 1872

In summer I lumberjack through Wisconsin.
Streams, ponds, cedar swamps, wells
dry up quicker than a culled Holstein.
Evergreens shed needles,
bristling the ground like a pricklepig.
Leaves stoke brush fires
started by loggers to burn slash,
and flare-ups dot the forest floor.

In Peshtigo, a saddlebag preacher predicts End Days,
concerned more with the fall of man than rainfall:
God's winnowing fan cleans the threshing floor,
and as He gathers wheat into the barn,
the chaff burns in unquenchable fire.
After passing the plate, he gallops off,
leaving us high on the Almighty
and dry from Sabbath temperance law.

For weeks, smoke blackens laundry on the line,
and hunters cannot sight game.
In a dry creek bed, one farmer digs six feet
before striking water for cows.
Whenever the Catholic Church bells sound
the alarm, villagers douse houses with buckets
of water from the Peshtigo River.
But like a cry wolf, the fires never advance.

Sunday, October 8, 1871.
At Vespers, we pray again for rain.
As the priest sprinkles holy water, he chants,

Deus, in adiutorium meum intende.
We believe God understands.

On the walk back home, the wind rises
and the western sky reddens.
As black snowflakes fall, the mutter of rainless thunder
grows to a roar, the earth trembles,
and fire drops from crimson sky.
Toward us speeds a tornado of flames!

As church bells clang, streets clog
with people in caps and gowns.
In the face of gale-force winds,
chimneys crumble, houses unroof,
and burning tree crowns whirl through the air
like skyrockets, setting fire to everything.
Some people burst into flames, votives,
going out moments later without prayer.

Like most folks, I run for the river.
Those stooping to bury treasures
incinerate, their places marked by ashen mounds.
In the stampede for the Peshtigo, some trample
the slower, while others pray for speed.
Many drown, especially children, disappearing
like stones skipped across roiled waters.
From chin-high current, I watch fire consume
the wooden-ware factory,
the gristmill, machine shop, sash factory,
the boarding house, and lumber camp.
The clangety-tang of tumbling bells
telegraphs the collapse of God's house.

Hours later, when the fires burn out,
I wade toward shore, slipping

on the skulls of sunken bodies.
On the river bank's hot sand, I fall asleep.

Next morning, the town looks like prairie
on the moon. I find dead horses,
oxen, cows, sheep, dogs, swine, chickens,
and people.
I discover the charred body of Emily,
or so says the engraved pie plate she carried
home from a church social.
When I come across a smothered girl
with lovely dark curls, I snip off a lock.
I don't know why.

The cremains of others wouldn't fill a fruit jar:
buckles, buttons, shawl pins, rings.
After I help some fellers carry bodies,
stacking them like so much kindling,
a woman, eyes black and dead as char,
points at the heap,
identifies each body by name, asks me,
Who the hell are you?

Days later, I tumble from funeral to funeral.
Mournful eyes of burned survivors glare,
my strangeness worth discussion
in whispers by the scarred and wounded,
my body without mark.

The first time I set myself on fire,
the lantern kerosene, a cool pool in my palm,
burned like incense to the dead
residing in my heart.

Their spirits speak to me
in tongues I cannot understand.
In an attempt to comprehend,
I burn my thigh with the orphaned coals
of a fireplace that closed its eyes to sleep.

One Sunday, I douse my body with lamp oil,
squat in the sacristy of the Catholic Church,
and beg the congregation to render a burnt offering.

STAFF ICEHOUSE WORKER: AMOS TANDY

We harvest in January,
when ponds and the West Fork freeze
thick enough to support horse and gig
to brush off snow.
In a red woolen shirt, vivid as a drowning man,
I square the ice field with groovers and gougers
into a quilt of glass.
While riding the shine-sleigh,
I sprinkle formaldehyde from the morgue
to clean off horse piss and shit.
Using a large-toothed one-man saw,
I cut blocks, horse-hauled to the icehouse.

In a yellow wooden barn-like building
with removable walls, we stack
true and deep and green,
using sawdust from our mill and salt hay
to insulate. I guarantee ice until September.

Throughout the asylum, every other day,
I trudge 25-pound blocks
with iron tongs and leather pad
slapped over my shoulder and, as needed,
to dairy farm and slaughterhouse.

I never married, cold feet,
cold hands,
cold as ice,
cold as a city girl's eyes,
cold as the crucified Christ.

It's agin' Mother Nature,
ice bobbing in tumblers of rum punch
in the middle of summer,

ones Dr. Ferguson offers his pet female
patient-of-the-day outside in the garden
where he fondles and kisses
while removing her bodice,
his chilling horselaugh
as I spy, hidden in the rhododendron,
breasts white as churned cream,
nipples brown as bread crust,
my body, flush, a glowing cookstove.

Sometimes, I lug a lunatic corpse
to the icehouse for storage
'til cemetery-thaw,
sometimes a female, embalmed,
the flimsy burial gown
sometimes open, the breasts
hard and firm, the nipples erect
in my mouth, brown and warm
as a fresh crust of bread.

DESERTION BY HUSBAND

```
W. Va. Hospital for the Insane
Name:     Hattie Wyatt
Admitted: 12 January, 1873
```

My ring on the floor,
spring rain plays a wedding waltz
as the tin roof leaks.

By lamplight shadow,
his enframed tintype glowers.
I shorten the wick.

Six children, one room.
Asleep, the youngest whimpers.
Cursed the fruit of womb!

Alone, I hunt the brute
with the pistol he forgot.
Only one bullet.

Grave consequences.
In the asylum, I sew
quilts from widow's weeds.

GUNSHOT WOUND

```
W. Va. Hospital for the Insane
Name:    William Fry
Admitted: 25 January, 1865
```

My church raises the $300
commutation fee in lieu of service,
but I want to see the world
Father finds so evil.

To prevent my leaving,
Father's hands clench the doorknob,
but Uncle Jack intervenes,
walks me two miles to the station,
leaves me with a poke of blackberry muffins
and one dollar, gold.
The train takes me to Youngstown
recruiting station where I ink
the company roll and leave description:
Height: 5'9"
Complexion: Fair
Occupation: Farmer.

A Mennonite, I am assigned
as steward in a field hospital.
Issued a gun to guard medical supplies,
morphine, opium, laudanum, and whiskey
stored in my wicker field knapsack,
I refuse to take possession.

All hours, I assist the surgeon:
bullet extractions, broken bones, amputations.
After skirmishes, I plod fifty feet to the next tent
and help the embalming surgeon.

After battles I whittle names on headboards,
lids from biscuit boxes,
marking shallow mass graves
where, days later, relatives exhume.

Once, due to theft, I watch a soldier writhe,
the boy's face, fevered-pink,
warm as a strangling-vined tomato,
flushed by a setting Ohio sun,
the sound of his last inward breath
like the swift snap off the vine.
To the family, I hand-deliver mementos
and, after returning to the front, I arm.

Midnight. The hospital tent.
Rummaging. The clink of bottles.
From under my pillow
I pull the revolver.
Toward the pilferer's shadow, I aim,
shout, *Who goes there?*
A bottle shatters across my forehead.
The firearm discharges.

———

In my room, the asylum doctor
scribbles scratchy in a notebook
as I, again and again, touch the doorknob
with my forehead, on the way to 500.
He speaks, *Mr. Fry. Mr. Fry, William.*
But I refuse to answer
until he addresses me proper:
Corporal James Weldon,
12th Regiment, Massachusetts Infantry,
6'2", dark complexion, wagon-maker.

When I returned from war, Mother,
poor soul, so rapt with homecoming,
she did not recognize me,
like the Christ transfigured,
like the resurrected Jesus.
Father equally confused,
cried, all the while drubbing me for
enacting this cruel impersonation
against mournful hearts.

FEMALE DISEASE

W. Va. Hospital for the Insane
Name: Daphne Hartz
Admitted: 27 April, 1866

When Daddy announces my arranged marriage
to the neighboring plantation owner,
a man he once described
as a foul-mouthed, mule-eared whoreson,
I run bawling to Mammy,
begging her to conjure Daddy out of it.
But she says, *Too late, chil'.*
De hoodoo take too long
and you too b'utiful.

———

Each evening, for hours I slave
to the stink of his body
and bear the vile engorgement of his lust
in joyless marital bondage.

When I believe I will break,
I run away to Mammy.
That night, hiding in her room,
I plead for help, saying
I'd rather be a gnarled tree,
my skin, thick bark, coarse as a rasp,
my limbs, rigid as knotty branches,
my hair, poisonous as sumac leaves

Like she's sighting game,
Mammy's eyes narrow.
Then a tree you be, she says.
By a tallow candle, we stitch a dress
of scratchy burlap, and weave

laurel leaves throughout the fabric.
In her conjuring gourd,
she mixes hog lard, red pepper, fox urine,
and dried poison ivy leaves.
Smear dis ober you, she says,
Fust he stay away from de smell,
den, when de rash come...
Mammy laughs.

Near dawn, my husband's hounds howl,
driven to frenzy by his curses and whip.
As I return through the swamp,
I drape my hair with moss clumps.
When he finds me, I pose like a cypress.

Despite the physician's repeated doctoring,
the pustules refused to heal.
When I nestle a bird's nest in my hair,
his Overseer returns me to Daddy
like a hessian sack of bad seed-potatoes.

———

Early in the war, my husband dies,
and bachelors disappear into conscription.
When the war ends, soldiers return,
dropping off their *carte de visite.*
Mammy and I shuffle through
the small photographic portraits,
giggling like twin Cupids.

In due time, to the one we favor,
I marry.
But in due time, he beats me,
carves his name in my trunk,
and like the tree in the Garden of Eden,

my eyes are opened. Beauty,
the source of the cross I bear,
like Wisdom, brings death.
Too ashamed to return home,
the twig is bent, and I petrify.

———

From my window in the asylum,
I see Mammy waiting for me
next to my sister, a sycamore
in bloom, her petals white as brides,
her arms opened wide,
beckoning me to reach for sky.

RELIGIOUS ENTHUSIASM

W. Va. Hospital for the Insane
Name: John Stanton
Admitted: 15 June, 1865

Bible in hand, a Dunkard preacher
led hymns, prayers, and laid hands, saying,
Where mankind are so reluctant to obey God,
they will not until they are excited!
Well, a woman paraded John up front
to the mourner's bench
where those in most need of salvation sat
next to the food: fried chicken, potatoes,
cob corn, and Lady Baltimore cake.
That's when he fell to the ground,
jerking and twitching like the St. Vitus,
not stopping 'til they tossed him in a pond,
baptizing him in front of trembling conscripts.

After the Battle of Tom's Brook,
when ordered to burn Rebel houses,
barns, fields, and farms, John declined
polite like, as if turning down a tea.
He spent the rest of the war in the stockade,
his forehead branded with a "C"
like a castrated bull.
I spent my days in shame,
his letters unopened. Of course,
the legislature passed my petition
for divorce from the coward.

After returning from the war, the prodigal
bawled like a weaning calf
in the face of my shotgun-backed *Git!*
Rejected by Baptists, Catholics, Protestants,

and every employer fit for a white man,
he took up preaching
his own brand of religion on street corners,
redeeming swaybacked horses and homeless
hounds. Denied a war pension,
he quit shaving, bathing, and converted
into a tumbleweed. One day he disappeared,
like maybe Jonah's whale swallowed him.

———

Months later, a traveling peddler,
mending my pie plates, tells me a tale
of some mad preacher
who attempted to walk on water
across the Ohio and ended up all wet,
flailing down river 'til fished out
and shored like driftwood.

SUPPRESSION OF MENSES

> W. Va. Hospital for the Insane
> Name: Anita Tanner
> Admitted: 10 January, 1882

I am
the woman at the well,
once winsome, tempting
as a branched apple.
Now, I am fruitless, without issue,
a seedless oddity,
a fallow field gone to weed
without savior, save for the crucified
husk-stuffed scarecrow.

I am
barren, a wormwood barn,
nesting ground for wasps,
twilight shadows, and decay,
useless as the broken
bits of whetstone lodged
in exhausted earth,
a crude mosaic tombstone
for the rusting scythe.

I am
an abandoned mill
shrouded by a moon without cycles,
chaff on the thresher's floor,
a dry riverbed
belly full of eroded stone.

I am
the lunatic who cuts herself,
legs spread, divining
for the confluent life
that once flowed.

STAFF LAUNDRY FOREMAN: OLIS CREMEANS

Tales of nuggets big as pinecones
lure me from livestock, friends, and seven kids,
and in January 1876, I travel
to the latest golden calf,
Whitewood Creek in the Black Hills,
what Lakota call
Womb of Mother Earth.

Twenty-five thousand gol' bugs
infest Indian Territory, settling claims
like saloon whores, with fists and forty-fives.
When my money is stoled,
I write home for a grubstake,
tell my woman, if she has to,
to steal from the church box.
I promised to return with gunnysacks
gorged with gold.
When I never hear back,
I do laundry for panners,
finding color in the bottom
of the wooden washtubs,
enough gold dust to hire a gaggle of laundress.

During the Sioux wars,
we follow Custer's army.
I scrub his uniforms myself.
To starve them into extinction
and to settle "the vexed Indian question,
General Sheridan orders,
Kill, skin, and sell 'til exterminated!
Custer asks, *Buffalo or Indian?*
The morning he rides out
toward the Little Big Horn,

his long hair glistens in the June sun,
the color of grass after a killing frost.

———

From the asylum lobby, I steal
a magazine for the shithouse.
For laughs, before tearing,
I read an interview
with some ignorant injun:

To save blood,
I want to show you my heart. Understand,
the Indian is not a wild animal.
Although the white man owns more words,
truth requires few.

The first white people, Lewis and Clarke,
brought guns, tobacco, and kindness.
We gave them horses.

For a while, peace reigned.

But then, white men found the yellow metal.
They stole our cattle, our horses, our land.
They lied for one another.
When we were not strong, they made war on us.

When we were strong
and the white men few,
we could have killed them all,
but all we ever wished for
was to live in peace.

After Chief Joseph, "An Indian's View of Indian Affairs," *North American Review*, April 1879.

EXPLOSION OF SHELL NEARBY

W. Va. Hospital for the Insane
Name: Isaac Mayhew
Admitted: 4 July, 1876

Over and over, like we is deaf
as harvested corn stalks, Granny warns
us to stay out of the battlefield:
If the haints don't get you, the duds will.
But even though battlefields is hallowed ground,
I still don't believe in ghosts,
and Cousin Joletta, she'd follow me anywhere
closer than a hound dog's shadow.

To celebrate the centennial, I aims
to make firecrackers from black powder
found inside unexploded bullets and cannon shells
left behind after the Battle of Shepherdstown
in the war of the sixties.
Last year, Mr. Darling, the blacksmith,
who brags he stood guard over Lincoln's casket,
set off two-inch bangers in his hands
like a fiery Greek god.
I resolve to outdo.

After church, Joletta meets me at Boteler's Ford
where we scavenge for 10-pound shells,
ones my Confederate uncle heard buzzing his ears,
sounding, he said, *Like Jesus planing wood.*
But when I salvage only ground-burst fragments,
good for nothing but slingshotting at crows,
I blame my cousin, call her Jonah
for all the bad luck she brung,

and cuss her to dig over yonder,
out of sight. She scats like a lame dog.

———

They drag my heels bloody into the asylum,
saying that the blast is what done it.
In my head, I hear voices
speaking in tongues like Pentecostals,
> *Like David, you sent her to the front line*
> *of battle, knowing she would die...*
The undertaker says that there is nothing left...
> *And if you smite her with an instrument of iron,*
> *so that she dies, you are a murderer...*
that Joletta's pickax hit the percussion fuse dead on...
> *No murderer has eternal life in him.*
that he don't understand my refusal to bear the pall,
seeing how I'm to blame, how he never seen a youngin'
so full of the devil and good for nothing
as when I attack the gravedigger
with his own pickax for spitting tobacco juice
in the fresh grave, while over and over, I yell,
That's hallowed ground!

TIME OF LIFE

W. Va. Hospital for the Insane
Name: Stephen Dunn
Admitted: 12 December, 1889

A time to scatter stones, a time to gather them.

Twelve, old enough, Pa says
to tote stone unearthed
while plowing virgin sod.
A crow, black as an undertaker,
perches on the limb of a dead oak
above turned earth while robins
prospect bug-teeming soil.
When Pa cusses a rock,
the mule brays, and the crow flies,
a solitary speck, swallowed
by a barren blue sky.

As I stack, I feel the burden.
Each rock weighs me down,
anchors me to my father's ways.
As I trace the horizon
of fence I mend each spring,
I spy the mule, pulling Pa,
his dead weight dragged
through a nest of copperheads.

Twelve, old enough, Ma says
to bear the pine with my uncles,
their necks chafed by starched collars;
old enough to bust sod, like Pa, stubborn
at first, but surrendering to the spade;
old enough to top the grave with stone
from fields I am old enough to man.

A time to be silent, a time to speak.

Ma cries when she sees me
in Pa's hemmed courtin' britches,
smelling of her cedar dowry chest.

All evening, silent as silk worms,
Mary Ellen Crowder and her mom
work on a yellow Easter gown
trimmed with English lace.
After reading the *Gazette* to shreds,
Mr. Crowder mutters he ain't wasting another candle.
As I watch him climb stairs to bed,
I clear my throat, but he doesn't stop.
Mrs. Crowder pokes me with a sewing needle.
My yelp catches the old man's attention:
Speak y'ur peace.
My voice cracks like a barn door
when I ask for Mary Ellen's hand.
He studies his daughter, blushing, staring
the varnish off the wood floor.
After glancing at his nodding wife,
he waves the folded newspaper and grunts.
Mother and daughter hug.
Crying, they run upstairs, passing the old man
who snarls, *'nough said.*

A time to kill, a time to heal.

In the crater of a cannon blast,
my rifle jams. As the enemy approaches,
I mount bayonet, play possum.
When I feel hands trying to remove my boots,
I thrust at a boy, maybe twelve,
his dirty face, bewildered. *Sorry, mister,*

he huffs, his hands holding his gut,
but I thought you was dead.
The boy falls at my feet.
To stop the bleeding, I wad my kerchief
inside the wound. Heaving the body
over my shoulder, I double-time it
to the rear of the line.

When I reach the surgeon's tent,
bloodstains confuse the steward;
we both get triaged.
Ain't nothin' wrong with you,
he snaps and spits chaw
toward a row of lifeless soldiers,
indicating where to lug the body.

As I squat beside the dead,
strung out like a mess of fish,
I wonder if it's right
to remove my kerchief. When two men
in blood-soaked aprons line up three more,
I stuff the sticky cloth in my pocket.
Hungry, I scrounge for something else to chew on.

A time to be born, a time to die.

After five pregnancies, I understand
a woman's need for things useful
after birth: diaper flannel, lamp filler,
ash pail, dishpan, wash basin.
In thirty minutes, I can build a fire
and provide the midwife with hot water,
enough for triplets. I use hickory,
a savory wood that smells like a growing home.

But that winter of Mary Ellen's sixth,
when a blizzard staves off womenfolk,
I figure I've witnessed enough births
to deliver: I know when to say, *Push,*
how to catch, how to tie the string,
cut the cord, wait for afterbirth.
A girl, Ellen, arrives, pretty
as a cask of two-penny nails.

But Mary Ellen won't stop bleeding.
By the time I rustle a doctor, he agrees
I done all I could, shakes my red hand,
dispenses condolences
and the name of a wet nurse.

Waiting for thaw, Mary Ellen sleeps
in the ice house
while I fill lamps, empty ash pail and dishpan,
line up wash basins,
and ready hot bath water for children,
enough for six.

A time to keep, a time to cast away.

A year after the burial, while I work
the fields, a stone's throw from the grave,
I arrange for a church woman
to sort through Mary Ellen's clothes.
Like a silent moth, I tell her to divest
the closet of every stitch Mary Ellen sewed.

That night, after tucking in the children,
I retire to bed. Through the gloom
of a half moon, in her vanity chair I see
her resurrected form, resplendent

in that yellow Easter gown
trimmed with English lace.
But when I call her name, *Mary Ellen*,
I realize my folly, understand the need
to keep a reminder of beauty
that succumbs neither to rot, rust, nor moth.

A time to mourn, a time to dance.

I give Ellen away to a young man
who dances like a foal finding its legs.
Pinned to her sleeve, something old
and borrowed, a ribbon of English lace.
For a while, we waltz.
After the music ends, I hear the swish
of her bridal gown in the corn broom
I use next day to sweep out her room.
Of habit, I fetch more wood
than needed to build a fire I will forget to tend,
and as the hearth grows cold,
by the dying light, I thread a needle
to restore a prodigal strip of English lace.

A time to embrace, a time to be far from embraces.

As I wait by the kitchen fireplace,
someone I don't know hugs me.
Rosa, the colored cook, tells me it's okay,
says the woman's name is Ellen.
Ellen asks me if I want to hug her.
I shake my head.
The woman cries, but I don't
see a wound. Maybe she's a new admission.

When Rosa asks me to lay a blaze
so she can warm her bunions,
that woman asks if she can watch.
Rosa nods. I think it queer.

As I start, Rosa adds,
What you doin', you 'splain to Miss Ellen.
Reluctant, I mutter, *Open the throat damper.*
Louder, Rosa says.
Check for an updraft!
More like it.

Maintain an inch-thick ash bed as an insulator.
On the andiron, set an 8-inch-diameter backlog
against the rear wall. Prevents brick cracking
and projects heat forward.
Then... I stop. I forget the next step.
I've started a thousand fires...

That woman tells me to set a 5-inch-diameter log
against the vertical holder of the andirons.
She's right. I do so but pretend I know and continue.
Between the logs place a handful of kindling.
To start the fire, use fatwood.
It has no pine-pitch to throw sparks.

The know-it-all chirps in,
Nature's one-match fire starter.

To maintain the fire, I advise,
use hardwoods: oak, cherry, maple...

Hickory's my favorite, she interrupts again.
But her eyes, dancing flames,
offer a comforting radiance, like a wife's
or daughter's.

Mine, too, I say. *It smells like...*
But my mind will not retrieve memory.
Like a growing home? she asks.
For a moment my mind resurrects.
I know this woman.
Yes, daughter, I say, *like a growing home,*
and Ellen smiles, starts to whimper.
But like a bobber floating on the water,
pulled under without warning,
my mind reels back into darkness.

As I start the fire, I let the odd woman
place her hand on my shoulder.
By the time flames leap like lake trout,
the lady's tears have dried
and I feel a familiar warmth.

ACKNOWLEDGMENTS

Anthology of Appalachian Writers (2009): "Grief"

International Psychoanalysis (2009): "Hereditary Predisposition,"
    "Loss of Leg," "Medicine to Prevent Conception"

Lady Jane's Miscellany (2009): "Women Trouble"

Off the Coast (2012): "Religious Excitement," "Sexual Abuse"

Sangam (2009): "Desertion by Husband"

Still: The Journal (2011): "WVa Hospital for the Insane," "Remorse,"
    "Suppression of Menses," "Staff Ice House Worker"

Survival Chronicles (2011): "Explosion of Shell Nearby"

*Cover art by Angela Nida (facebook.com/angela.nida); cover execution and
interior book design by Diane Kistner (dkistner@futurecycle.org); Adobe
Caslon Pro text with Courier titling and admission loggings.*

ABOUT FUTURECYCLE PRESS

FutureCycle Press is dedicated to publishing lasting English-language poetry and flash fiction books, chapbooks, and anthologies in both print-on-demand and ebook formats. Founded in 2007 by long-time independent editor/publishers and partners Diane Kistner and Robert S. King, the press incorporated as a nonprofit in 2012. A number of our editors are distinguished poets and authors in their own right, and we have been actively involved in the small press movement going back to the early seventies.

The FutureCycle Poetry Book Prize and honorarium is awarded annually for the best full-length volume of poetry we publish in a calendar year. We are dedicated to giving all authors we publish the care their work deserves, making our catalog of titles the most distinguished it can be, and paying forward any earnings to fund more great books.

We've learned a few things about independent publishing over the years. We've also evolved a unique, resilient publishing model that allows us to focus mainly on vetting and preserving for posterity the most books of exceptional quality without becoming overwhelmed with bookkeeping and mailing, fundraising activities, or taxing editorial and production "bubbles." To find out more about what we are doing, come see us at www.futurecycle.org.